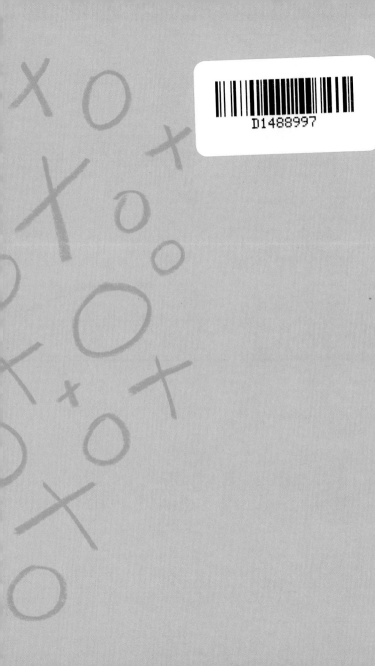

LOVE IS ♡
LOVE
IS LOVE
IS LOVE
IS LOVE

LOVE

is... PARADISE

WHEN ASKED FOR HIS DEFINITION OF PARADISE:

"THIS MORNING,
WITH HER,
HAVING COFFEE."

_johnny_cash_ ♡♡

LOVE is...

soul

FOR IT WAS NOT
INTO MY EAR
YOU WHISPERED,
BUT INTO MY HEART.
IT WAS NOT MY
LIPS YOU KISSED,
BUT MY SOUL.

♡ judy garland

LOVE is...

pers

istent.

THE BEST thing
TO hold ONTO
in LiFE is
each other.

♡ audrey ♡
hepburn

LOVE IS...

wri

WE'RE ALL A LITTLE
weird. AND
LIFE IS A LITTLE WEIRD.
AND WHEN WE
FIND someone
WHOSE WEIRDNESS
IS COMPATIBLE
WITH OURS,

WE JOIN UP
WITH THEM AND
fall into
MUTUALLY SATISFYING
weirdness—
AND call it love.

robert fulghum ♡

love is...

LOYAL

LOVE IS *absolute*

PEOPLE **FADE**

BUT
LOYALTY NEVER

YOU CAN DEPEND SO MUCH

YOU CAN SET YOUR

AND *that's love*

Sylvester

loyalty.

LOOKS FADE,

FADES.

ON CERTAIN PEOPLE;

WATCH BY THEM

EVEN IF IT DOESN'T

SEEM VERY exciting.

stallone

LOVE IS...

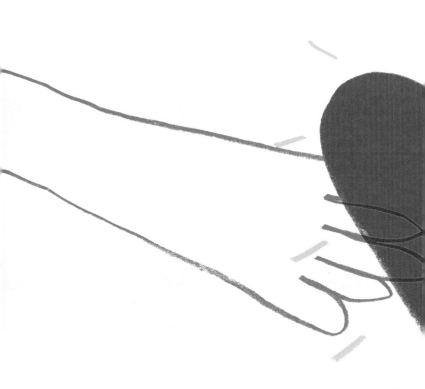

PEACE
FUL

Love never
claims,
it _ever_ gives.

Love ever suffers,
never resents,
never revenges
itself.

Gandhi

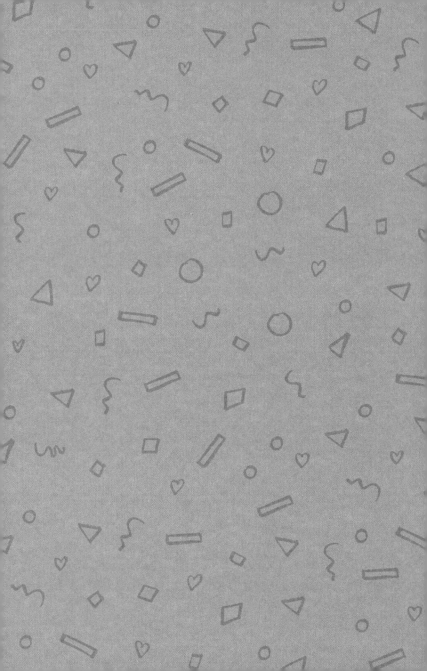

IN ALL *the world,*
there is NO HEART
for me like

YOURS.

IN ALL *the world,*
there is no LOVE
for you like

MINE.

MAYA ANGELOU

Love is...

PASSi

ONATE

LOVE IS
LIKE
friendship
CAUGHT ON FIRE.
IN THE BEGINNING
A *flame,*
VERY PRETTY,
OFTEN HOT
AND *fierce,*

BUT STILL *light* AND *flickering.*

AS LOVE GROWS OLDER,
OUR HEARTS MATURE
AND OUR LOVE
BECOMES AS COALS,
DEEP-BURNING AND
unquenchable.

♡ BRUCE LEE

LOVE is...

oVERWHEL

I was,
AND AM,

swept away

I BELIEVE THERE
ARE SOME THINGS
YOU CAN'T DENY OR
RATIONALIZE,

AND THIS *is one*
of them. ♡♡

Cate
Blanchett

LOVE IS...
comPROMiSE

TRUE *love* is...

SINGING KARAOKE "UNDER PRESSURE" AND LETTING THE OTHER PERSON SING THE FREDDIE MERCURY PART.

mindy kaling

ALL YOU NEED IS LOVE.
BUT A LITTLE

chocolate

NOW + THEN
DOESN'T HURT.

charles Schulz

LOVE IS...

ten

der

The
REAL LOVER
is the MAN
who can
THRILL YOU
by KISSING your
FOREHEAD.

MARILYN MONROE ♡

LOVE is...

JOYFUL

Love is a
FRIENDSHIP
set to
MUSIC.

joseph ♥
campbell

LOVE iS...

everything ♡

I LOVE HER,

and that's the
BEGINNING
and
END
OF EVERYTHING.

♡ F. Scott Fitzgerald

LOVE IS...

team
work
♡

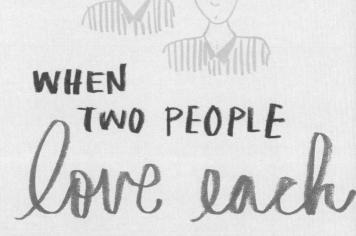

WHEN
TWO PEOPLE
love each

THEY DON'T LOOK AT
EACH OTHER,
THEY LOOK IN
THE same

other

direction.

GINGER ROGERS

Everything
IS CLEARER
WHEN
YOU'RE IN
LOVe.

john
Lennon

Published by Sourcebooks, Inc.
P.O. Box 4410, Naperville, Illinois 60567-4410
(630) 961-3900
Fax: (630) 961-2168
sourcebooks.com

Printed and bound in China.
QL 10 9 8 7 6 5 4 3 2 1